HARROW
A Pictorial History

METRO-LAND

PRICE TWO-PENCE

HARROW
A Pictorial History

Dennis F. Edwards

Phillimore

1993

Published by
PHILLIMORE & CO. LTD.,
Shopwyke Manor Barn, Chichester, Sussex

ISBN 0 85033 874 3

Printed and bound in Great Britain by
BIDDLES LTD.
Guildford, Surrey

List of Illustrations

Frontispiece: Cover from Metropolitan
Railway guide book, 1930

Introduction

The name of Harrow is known all over the world. The spire of St Mary's church rising above its girdle of trees up on the hill is one of the most prominent landmarks of Middlesex. The steep streets and the long High Street, with its groups of School buildings, have an old-fashioned atmosphere; it is almost as if most of the 20th century has passed unheeded.

Harrow conjures up the great names of the past; Palmerston, Byron and Churchill. Yet today, in the last decade of the 20th century, the name Harrow means more than the School. It is a vast modern suburb of what is the London Borough of Harrow, incorporating the old villages of Pinner and Stanmore, and Victorian Wealdstone, the product of the railway age. This book is a collection of pictures illustrating the growth of Harrow and district over the last 100 years.

Early History

Harrow was first recorded in A.D. 767 when King Offa made a grant of land in the neighbourhood of the hill. The place name was written as 'Gum eninga hergae', which means a clearing or sacred grove of the Gumne, a local tribe. Later, the name was adapted by the Normans as Harwo, although the name often appears in early documents as Hergra.

Were the Romans here before them? There is no evidence of Roman settlement at Harrow, but certainly they were at Brockley Hill, Stanmore. Here the Romans had an important pottery conveniently sited along the main road to St Albans – Watling Street – now the modern Edgware Road. The settlement was called Sulloniacae. There is also evidence of Roman times at Bentley Priory, Stanmore. In 1781 estate workers found a hoard of Roman coins and ornaments. On Stanmore Common, one of the ponds was at one time known locally as Caesar's Pond, and an earthwork nearby, Caesar's Fort. But the rest of the Harrow area was one of dense forest and scrub. Hugh Thomson in his *Highways and Byways in Middlesex* (1909) quotes a local verse: 'No hear can think, nor tounge can tell/ What lies between Brockley Hill and Perivale'. Today the answer would be 'miles of concrete and brick!'.

We are more certain of historical fact about St Mary's church on Harrow Hill. In 1094 the Archbishop of Canterbury commissioned a church, but it was left to his successor, St Anselm, to carry out the consecration. However, the Bishop of London, Lanfranc, felt he was being snubbed and there was an unseemly disturbance during the ceremony. Quite substantial parts of this church remain, including the lower parts of the tower. The nave was rebuilt in the 13th century whilst the fine timber roof and famous spire were added in the 15th century, the spire dating from *c*.1459. The chancel dates from the 14th century. There is a pulpit of 1675 although it was not installed until 1708. In common with many Middlesex churches, St Mary's had become rather dilapidated by the end of the 18th century. A correspondent in the *Gentlemen's Magazine* in 1786 wrote that the chancel was in such a state that it was a dangerous structure. Between 1841-49 the great restoration under Sir George Gilbert Scott took place. Scott encased the external walls in flint and added the North Chapel in addition to other improvements. Harrow grew very slowly in the Middle Ages. The most important manor in the area was at Headstone. The existing moated Manor and house date from the 14th century and Thomas [ac]a Becket is said to have spent his last Christmas at the Manor. Certainly, it has been associated with the Archbishops of Canterbury until recent times.

On the hill itself, the settlement had grown sufficiently for a market to be granted in 1226, but apparently it did not flourish and had died out by the 16th century. The inhabitants of the old, quiet town experienced much excitement (and some alarm) in January 1524. A long procession arrived: carts bearing all kinds of things, boats and pack horses with food and a long column of churchmen and merchants – friends of the Prior of St Bartholomew in Smithfield, London. The prior had had a vision that all London was to be flooded on 1 February, so he had a wooden tower built on the hill in the grounds of what is now The Grove. But the day came and went and nothing happened. A few weeks later the Prior and his retinue returned to London rather shame-faced. Harrow Hill has so often been compared to an island – its boundary fields the foreshores and the lands of the plain the sea!

The Manor of Harrow was granted in 1545 by Archbishop Cranmer to Henry VIII. The king later granted the Manor to Sir Edward North, whose family held it until 1630. The Manor (with its sub-manors of Woodall (Pinner), Headstone and Roxeth) passed to Edmund Phillips and subsequently to George and Rowland Pitt. In 1797, one of the Pitt daughters married James Rushout. He was later created Lord Northwick. The Northwicks only lived in their house on Harrow Hill until 1812, after which they moved to their estate at Blockley, near Moreton-in-Marsh, Gloucestershire. The family continued to own land in Harrow for another century. Just before the First World War, Lord Northwick sold the land for housing development. Northwick Park station opened in 1923 to serve the new district and many of the roads are named after the family, for example, Rushout Avenue, Churchill Avenue.

Here is what John Norden, writing in his book *Speculum Britanniae* in 1593, said about Harrow:

It may be noted how nature hath exulted that high Harrow-on-the-Hill, as it were in the way of ostentation to show it selfe to all passengers to and from London, who beholding the same maye say it is the centre (as it weer) of the pure vale: for Harrow stands invironed with a great contrye of moste pure ground from which hill, towards the time of harvest, a many maye beholde the fyldes round about ... so sweetly to address tthemselves to the sicle and syth, with such comfortable abundanc of all kinde of grayne ...

It was in this period that a middle-class landowner or yeoman, John Lyon, was farming in the hamlet of Preston. In 1572 he obtained a charter from Elizabeth I to found a school for local boys in the small town of Harrow. It is believed that he chose Harrow because there may already have been some kind of educational establishment there. He made practical provisions for the buildings, including 'Meete and convenient rooms for the said schoolmaster and usher to inhabit and dwell in :and also a large and convenient school house, with a chimney in it'. Lyon also stated that the Master 'to be on no account below the degree of a mastre of arts'. Although he intended the school to be for local scholars, there was a provision for 'foreigners'. Lyon died on 11 October 1592, and so did not live to see his school flourish. He is commemorated by a fine brass in St Mary's.

Certainly the school began to flourish in its early days, but gradually the numbers of local places fell as more and more scholars from places far and wide arrived. Eventually, free places for local boys were abolished under the Public School Act of 1868. However, Lyon's bequest was not forgotten. The Lower school of John Lyon was founded in 1876 and is a flourishing establishment today.

Life at Harrow School two centuries or more ago was not pleasant. Pupils lived and studied under very harsh conditions. Sport was of a rough nature, like hunting, and even the famous Silver Arrow archery contests attracted rowdy scenes. Not all riots were between rival school factions; there were many cases of the boys attacking local inhabitants, particularly on Saturday nights when the farm workers arrived in town to spend the evening at taverns like the old *Crown and Anchor*, which stood at the foot of Church Hill. It was outside such a place as this that young Anthony Ashley Cooper (later Lord Shaftesbury) was so appalled at the scenes connected with a pauper's funeral that he decided to devote his life to aiding the under-privileged. There is a commemorative plaque to him on the wall of the Old Schools building. His national memorial is in Piccadilly Circus – the statue on the top is of Eros. Crown Street, once called Hog Lane, was the scene of many fights between the scholars and the rougher elements of the town. But some of the disturbances were directed at the School Authorities. In 1771, for example, pupils objecting to the appointment of Dr. Benjamin Heath set fire to the coach belonging to one of the School Governors. In 1805, however, there was a more dangerous crisis: when Dr. George Butler succeeded Dr. Joseph Drury, gun-powder was used in an attempt to blow up a building which he was visiting.

Dr. Butler was headmaster until 1829. He began the series of reforms that were to make Harrow world famous. The Old Schools were expanded and partly reconstructed, and he raised the standard of classical scholarship. Yet he failed to stem the decline in the numbers attending, and by 1845 there were only 69 boys. Under the headships of Dr. Charles Vaughan (1845-1859) and Dr. Henry Montagu Butler (1860-1885) the School was transformed. A separate chapel was built in 1837, which was succeeded by Scott's impressive building of 1857. The Vaughan Library was added in 1862, followed by the Butler Museum (1886), the Speech Room (1877) and the Art School by the end of the Victorian period.

In the early 19th century, farming began to prosper and more shops opened in the old town. Various trades serving the local farmers – saddlers, wheelwrights and farriers – flourished. The majority of the people on the Hill were engaged in activities serving the School such as laundry work, tailoring, shoe-making, catering and straw hat cleaning. From 1824 there was a daily coach service to London from outside the *King's Head Hotel*. Most of the expansion of Harrow in early Victorian times was to the west, down the Hill to Roxeth and along the Northolt Road.

Roxeth is first mentioned as far back as A.D. 845, recorded as 'Hroc'. Derivations of the name are found locally in Roxbourne and Roxborough. The name may also mean 'rook's place'. Up to the Roxeth Enclosure Act of 1817, the area consisted of open common land, marshy in places (Roxeth Marsh). There were a few large farms – Grange Farm (with moat and great barn), St Hilda's Farm, and Roxborough Farm among others. Roxeth Farm still survives as a private house at the junction of Besborough Road and Whitmore Road. In the 19th century Roxeth Fields were important for the growing of hay crops. The hay was in great demand to feed the ever-increasing numbers of London horses. The suburb grew slowly, industrialisation arriving in 1856 with the building of the gas works, although coal had to be brought from Wealdstone station. The works was considerably expanded after the formation of the Harrow District Gas Company in 1873, and by the 1930s was supplying most of the rapidly growing districts of Greater Harrow. It was a structure much disliked by residents of Harrow and Roxeth, and with its prevailing smell of gas it became one of the most unpleasant areas of Harrow. The gas works were connected by rail to the Metropolitan railway at Rayners Lane from 1904. The huge gas holder was at last dismantled a few years ago and the manufacture of gas ceased at Roxeth.

Roxeth parish church was consecrated in 1862. The Cottage Hospital opened in 1906, replacing an earlier establishment, and was described at the time as 'the most perfect little hospital in England'. After the First World War, there was an ever-increasing amount of building activity and by 1939 Roxeth had been linked with West Harrow, Rayners Lane and Northolt Park. On 6 May 1833 the London and Birmingham railway was authorised to start work on the world's first long-distance railway. Plans for a line had been formulated as early as 1823 and a survey was made for a route to pass along the foot of the Harrow Weald heights. Robert Stephenson was appointed engineer for the London and Birmingham company and lands were purchased from Lord Northwick, New College, Oxford as well as Hatch End Farm at Pinner Park. It was at the latter that Joseph Nowell, the contractor, set up his local construction base. The land later became the site of the Commercial Traveller's School.

The 'navigators' constructing the line were not popular. Fighting in local public houses was common. The *Queen's Arms*, in what is now Wealdstone, at times had so many patrons that the landlord had to ladle ale from pails to the crowds outside. One local resident described the navvies as 'Banditti, possessing all the daring recklessness of the smuggler ... without any of the redeeming qualities'. Even the scholars from the great School joined in the fun, riding illegally on the waggons and narrow gauge track used by the contractors. More seriously, they engaged in throwing stones at the navvies – who, despite their fearsome reputation as fighters, often came off the losers. Eventually disciplinary action was taken by Dr. Christopher Wordsworth, the headmaster at that time.

There was a trial trip for Directors and friends from Euston to the temporary terminus at Boxmoor on 29 June 1837. This was followed by a series of what we would now describe as 'test trains'. The first passenger train to Boxmoor was on Thursday 20 July 1937. The first through train from London to Birmingham ran on 17 September 1838. The line was highly praised: '...a piece of human workmanship of the most stupendous kind, which when considered with respect to its scientific character, magnitude, utility, its harmony of arrangement, and mechanical contrivance, eclipses all former works of art'.

The station at Wealdstone was opened (as Harrow Weald station) on 20 July 1837. A master at the School, W. W. Phelps, recorded in his diary for 31 July: 'First saw train on the railroad at the Weald'. A few days later he again writes: 'It is a great diversion to go down to the railroad station and see the arrival of a train. We saw about four hundred persons brought up at the rate of 32 miles per hour by one train and engine'. But not everybody in Harrow was pleased. The Vicar of St Mary's complained to the London and Birmingham railway about the practice of running trains on Sundays.

The School governors wanted a station at the point where the Harrow Road crossed the new line at what is now Wembley – probably because the road was in a better state of repair than muddy Greenhill Lane to 'Harrow Weald' station. The more articulate residents of Pinner wanted a station at Dove House Bridge (Hatch End). Stations were opened at these two places in 1842. There were also a few all too modern complaints about the regularity of the local train service and the high fares. Guide book writers were soon at work describing the delights of rail travel. *Lloyds Guide to the London and Birmingham Railway* states: 'On the left of the road is the town of Harrow so celebrated for its School at which many of our most distinguished statesmen were educated. Harrow Weald station is the first halting place on the line, is about eleven miles and a quarter from London'.

The novelty of train travel and the attractions that could be visited en route soon brought visitors to Harrow. On 7 August 1838, a party came by train to Harrow Weald and one passenger, Thomas Port, father of John Port, hat manufacturer of Burton-upon-Trent, was run over by a locomotive and his legs were badly injured. Had he been 'larking about' with his friends? He died later that day and his sorrowing father erected a large slate memorial stone by the porch at Harrow church. The epitaph is so typical of the style of that age:

Bright rose the morn and vic'rous rose poor Port
Gay on the train, he used his wanted sport:
'Er noon arrived, his mangled form they bore,
With pain distorted and o'er whelmed with gore.
When evening came to close that fatal day, A mutilated corpse the suffer lay.

The London and Birmingham Railway and its successor, The London and North Western, was more concerned with fast trains to the Midlands and the north than local traffic. The few local trains that called at Hatch End (then called Pinner) delayed the start of any housing developments for many years.

Harrow Weald station changed its name to Wealdstone by the end of the 1830s. There was a Wealdstone House and Farm and gradually the area around the station became known as Wealdstone. The first sale of local land for housing development was in 1859 when part of the Headstone Farm lands was sold – some 500 acres. Two roads were laid out: Pinner Drive (soon renamed Headstone Drive) and Harrow View. By way of encouragement to prospective residents, the railway offered cheap travel: 'To every occupier of a new house above £50 rent, a gift of an 11 year ticket to Euston'. Prospective residents in the new areas were assured of the 'privileges accorded to residents in respect of Harrow School are of themselves sufficient to give the locality respectability'.

Wealdstone was very much a product of the Victorian railway age. Yet there had been a small hamlet called Weald Stone at least since the 18th century when it is so named in John Rocque's *New and Accurate Map of the Country adjacent to the Cities* (published in 1754). His map of the Weald Stone (the name did not become one word until the mid-19th century) also shows the hill known as Bell Mount – present-day Belmont. Wealdstone takes its name from the ancient marker stone which can be seen outside the *Red Lion* at Harrow Weald, and there is a reference to 'Weld Ston' in a document of the 16th century. The stone is now accepted as having been a parish marker between Harrow and the forested area of Harrow Weald. By the time the London and Birmingham railway was built in the 1880s, the name Wealdstone was in general use despite efforts of early housing-estate developers to call the area Harrow Park or simply Station End (the station was called Harrow). It was at this time that industry began to arrive. Kodak Limited was established in 1891 on a seven-acre site off Headstone Drive. The new factory had its own artesian wells and a power station. The present factory now covers 55 acres. Winsor and Newton, manufacturers of artists' materials, arrived in 1897 followed by Hamilton Brushes in 1898, moving from Clerkenwell. Whitefriars Glass works also came from the city at this time. A number of printing works also followed including H.M. Stationery Office Printing Works.

Roads of terraced houses began to branch out from the High Street and their names reflect the popular heroes of the period: Peel, Cannon, Palmerston, Grant, Cecil, Havelock Roads and many others. In 1881 there were 211 houses and by 1911 there were 2,567. The Wealdstone Urban District Council was formed in 1894, lasting until the reorganistion of local government in 1933 when it merged with Harrow Urban District Council.

The new station at Pinner (Hatch End) attracted some building, particularly on the Woodriddings estate. One row of large Italianate properties was called Chandos Villas and Mr. and Mrs. Samuel Beeton made their home from 2 August 1856 to 1862 at number 2. It was here that Isabella wrote her famous book of household management which was published in her husband's magazine. There was also a plan to lay out an estate of high-class villas at Brickfields on Harrow Hill. The proposer was Charles Laws, whose father was proprietor of the *King's Head*.

But the development of Harrow really began with the arrival of the Metropolitan Railway in 1880. The railway extended from Willesden Green and the official opening date was Saturday 31 July: the first public trains began the following Monday. The engineer for the line was Charles Liddell, whose niece was Alice of 'Wonderland' fame. The railway was also planned to go on to Pinner in 1885, Chesham (1889) and eventually Aylesbury (1892). The local press commented when the work was under way: 'The Harrow railway will pass close to the property of Harrow School. There will probably be a passenger station near it'.

The site for Harrow-on-the-Hill station was on the Lowlands estate. This had been the seat of Benjamin Rotch (1793-1854), local businessman and benefactor. He had established all kinds of novelties on the estate including hydropathic baths. The grounds were landscaped and planted with many rare trees, including a giant Judas Tree. His widow, Isabella Rotch, had a long life. When she died at Lowlands on 22 April 1909 (aged 100), Harrow had changed dramatically. Eventually the remaining part of the estate became a school (now Greenhill College) and part of the grounds a public park.

The opening of the Metropolitan was celebrated with a lunch for 250 people at the *King's Head Hotel* and amongst those present were Sir Edward Watkin, Chairman of the Metropolitan, H. D. Pochin (Deputy Chairman), B. Whitworth M.P., Lord Alfred Churchill and Sir Morton Peto. Above the guests was a banner proclaiming 'Stet Fortuna Domus' – let the house remain prosperous – the Latin no doubt lost on the new residents but it impressed the School Governors. Sir Edward Watkin proposed the Loyal Toast and the Deputy Headmaster proposed the School. Lord Churchill proclaimed: 'This extension is the first attempt of the Metropolitan to put its claws out of the Metropolise [sic]'. The new station was in Queen Anne-style and the *Harrow Observer* reported that it was 'Designed to have character and dignity in keeping with the Town and its Associations ... the booking office, waiting rooms have walls faced with enamelled bricks and adorned with stained glass windows and painted dados'. The main station buildings were approached via a short turning from Lowlands Road, there being just a narrow footpath on the north side into the quiet residential street called College Road. How different from today! Residents of Harrow were offered a free return trip to Willesden Green on the first day of public opening. The expansion of Greenhill, the hamlet along the lane between the Hill and Wealdstone, began to accelerate.

In 1882 a writer for the magazine *All the Year Round* reported: 'Soon the road between Paddington and Harrow will become one long high street. Clearly, Harrow is destined to become suburban'. And again: 'There is a demand for villa type houses which at present cannot be met by local builders'. There was a further impetus to the future expansion of Harrow when the Metropolitan opened the branch line from Harrow-on-the-Hill to Uxbridge in 1904.

The District Railway's Ealing and South Harrow line opened in 1903, with a station near the Northolt Road on the edge of Roxeth. The terminus was called South Harrow Halt for Roxeth and Northolt. Electric trains did not begin running over the Roxeth viaduct to Rayners Lane until 1910 due to legal difficulties with the Metropolitan Railway. On the L.N.W.R. line, work was completed in 1913 with the provision of two extra suburban tracks from London to Watford – the New Lines. Steam trains began a greatly improved suburban timetable from Monday 10 February and a new station was opened at Headstone Lane, and also at Kenton, whilst Wealdstone and Hatch End were rebuilt. Electric tube trains from the Bakerloo Railway began running through to Watford on 16 April 1917. On 20 July 1922 the L.N.W.R. electric service from Euston and also Broad Street began. By 1914 Harrow was already expanding and the quiet Greenhill Lane had become busy Station Road with parades of shops and side roads of smart villas. Harrow Weald still retains much open space – its wooded hills marking the northern boundary between Middlesex and Hertfordshire. In his book on Middlesex, published in 1816, J. Norris Brown described the area and the origins of its name:

> ...an allusion to its former umbrageous and rural character, the term Weald signifies in the Saxon, a wood. The wide range of land possesses some fine inequalities of surface, and at many points are obtained rich and diversified projects.

The fine views appreciated in the early 19th century are still enjoyed, especially the famous view from the car park in Old Redding near *The Case is Altered*.

One of the 18th-century residents of Harrow Weald was a landowner named Daniel Dancer (1716-1794). He possessed a fortune, but for many years lived with his sister in an increasingly decrepit house, spending the minimum amount of money possible. He became famous as one of the great misers of history. When he died a fortune was found, buried in the garden and hidden in the chimney – a hiding place he favoured because he never had a fire.

By the Victorian period Harrow Weald was renowned for its large houses set amid the woods and plantations. One famous local family was the Blackwell family. They lived at various houses in the area, including The Cedars along the road to Hatch End (demolished in 1957 for a council estate). It was Thomas Blackwell who, in 1819, linked with his friend Edmund Crosse to form the famous food company. Crosse lived in Clamp Hill. Both partners are buried at Harrow Weald church. The district's most famous resident was Sir William Gilbert of Gilbert and Sullivan fame. His house was Grimsdyke, designed by Norman Shaw for the artist Frederick Goodall. Sir William and Lady Gilbert planted many ornamental trees and shrubs in the grounds. In 1911, Gilbert died of a heart attack whilst attempting to rescue a girl who had got into difficulties whilst swimming in the lake. Gilbert is buried in the churchyard of Stanmore church. Harrow Weald parish church dates from 1846; the architects were J. J. Harrison and William Butterfield. In 1890 Butterfield designed the tower, the last commission the distinguished architect undertook before his death. In the churchyard is the grave of Captain W. Leefe Robinson V.C., the first man to shoot down a Zeppelin in the First World War.

Stanmore, as mentioned earlier, takes its name from the Roman settlement of Sulloniacae. Modern Stanmore is actually two places: Great (or Magna) Stanmore and Little Stanmore (Parva). It was at Little Stanmore that James Brydges (1673-1744) purchased the old estate of Canons and set about building a vast and lavishly decorated house in the early part of the 18th century. He had been paymaster general to the army and navy between 1707-11 and made a fortune in the American Colonies. It was the 1st Duke of Chandos that he commissioned James Gibb to build Canons, which Defoe called 'The most magnificent mansion house in England. It was a palace of lakes, statues and landscaped garden splendour. Most of the great figures of the time paid the Duke visits. Pope was a frequent guest – every servant is made easy and his life comfortable'. The Duke had a resident orchestra and his master of music was the great Handel himself. For the beautifully decorated Little Stanmore church, Handel composed the Chandos anthems. All London marvelled at the grounds, where amid the fine statues and temples a live tiger wandered about. After the Duke's death the estate had to be sold and its contents scattered, the great mansion itself being demolished. The site was purchased by William Hallett in 1747 and a new house built. The mansion and grounds are now the North London Collegiate School. Pope seems to have foreseen the end of the great days of Canons:

> Grove nods at grove, each alley has a brother
> and half the platform just reflects the other
> The suffering eye invented nature sees
> Trees cut to statues, statues thick as trees ...
> ... another age shall see the golden ear
> Imbrown the slope, and nod on the partere
> Deep harvest bury all his pride has plan'd
> And laughing Ceres re-assume the land.

That 'age' was to be the 1930s and the 'imbrowning harvest' (that of bricks and mortar) the vast housing estates of the inter-war years.

Defoe mentions that in the neighbourhood were 'a great many very beautiful seats of the nobility and gentry'. That other explorer in the district, J. Norris Brown, mentions that the church of Great Stanmore had a tower 'richly enveloped in a profusion of ivy. The porch was designed by Nicholas Stone, who received thirty pounds ... the east window is filled with stained glass of gaudy colours and by no means eminent for beauty.' The red-brick church he saw is only an empty but picturesque ruin today. It was built in 1632 by Sir John Wolstenholme to replace the ruined medieval church which was located on a slightly different site. By the early years of Victoria's reign, the church was becoming unsafe. The foundation stone of the present church was laid on 14 March 1849 by the 4th Earl of Aberdeen, who gave £2,000 towards the new building. Amongst those present was Queen Adelaide, widow of William IV.

Lord Aberdeen was Prime Minister between 1852 and 1855 and is buried at Stanmore. His coffin was recently rediscovered during research work at the old church. The new church was consecrated on 16 January 1850. The east window is in memory of Queen Adelaide who died shortly after the new church was consecrated. The Queen's last home was at Bentley Priory, which was designed by Sir John Soane and built between 1789 and 1798 by James Hamilton (later Marquess of Abercorn). The lengthy period for the building work was due to the eccentric requests and constant alterations that the Marquess demanded. Later, Sir Robert Smirke added further work and, by the time Queen Adelaide had acquired the house, it was considerably altered yet again. She died there on 2 December 1849. Sir John Kelk the engineer was the next owner. In 1882 the property was purchased by Frederick Gordon, the famous hotelier. Gordon converted the building into a luxury country hotel and advertised it in 1882 thus:

> Bentley Priory is now open for use as a luxury country hotel ... the distance from London is a little over ten miles by a good carriage road, carriages or private omnibuses from the hotel may be ordered for any train. A well-appointed coach leaves the Metropole and Grand hotels every morning (Sunday excepted) returning in good time in the evening.

The hotels mentioned were owned by Gordon and stood in Northumberland Avenue in London. Frederick Gordon felt, however, that a direct railway connection would be better for trade. He obtained an Act of Parliament on 28 June 1888 for a branch line from Harrow and Wealdstone station to a terminus near Stanmore church. Work began on 27 July 1889 when Miss Gordon cut the first sod. There was an official opening on Thursday 18 December 1890 which turned out to be a bitterly cold day. The *Harrow Observer* reported:

> The weather was not in the best mood. The cold was rather severe and some fog hung about, but the many who had repaired to the London and North Western Railway at Harrow (Wealdstone) to take the train to Stanmore, appeared to be in good spirits, as if in anticipation of the good cheer before them ... the 12.17 train from Harrow was soon full, and after a short and smooth runover the newly constructed line, the merry freight discharged at Stanmore station, where the

music of the Harrow town brass band welcomed passengers. Several closed carriages were in waiting, in which guests were taken to Bentley Priory. As the corner of the village was passed, the church bells could be heard merrily ringing out.

The L.N.W.R. operated the railway, but although it was used by the villagers, it did not improve trade at the Priory. Gordon closed the hotel but continued to live there in splendour: after all, he had been called 'The Napoleon of the hotel world'. In 1925 the Air Ministry purchased the property and in the Second World War it became the headquarters of Fighter Command. The building was badly damaged by fire some years ago.

Stanmore grew only slowly before 1914. The branch was fairly well used and on 12 September 1932 an intermediate station was opened at Belmont. Stanmore station closed to passengers on 15 September 1952 although goods traffic continued until 6 July 1964. Belmont then became the terminus until it closed on 5 October 1964.

Great developments were to come to Stanmore at the beginning of the 1930s with the arrival of the Metropolitan Railway from Wembley Park via Kingsbury and Canons Park. When plans were announced in 1929, Stanmore residents were not particularly pleased. They feared that the fields and quiet parklands to the south of the village would be developed. The Metropolitan agreed to plant the cuttings and embankments of the new line with trees and shrubs. The line was financed by the Government Loans and Guarantees and Grants Act 1929, which was aimed at helping the unemployed. The contractor was Walter Scott and Middleton and work began on 1 April 1931, with a scheduled completion date of September 1932, but heavy clay in two wet summers and the need to divert the Wealdstone brook delayed the work. The railway opened on 9 December 1932. Stations were opened at Kingsbury, Canons Park (which was originally to be called Whitchurch Lane) and Stanmore. Queensbury station did not open until 19 December 1934 to serve the rapidly expanding estates in the Honeypot Lane area.

By 1939, almost all the open land south of Canons Park had become covered in houses, and it was only the outbreak of war plus Harrow's plans to preserve the attractive countryside in the Harrow Weald and Stanmore area that stopped the suburbs spilling over the border into Hertfordshire. For the two decades between the end of the First World War and the beginning of the Second World War rural Middlesex was almost completely drowned under a great tide of housing estates. This was the age of Metroland. At the end of that remarkable period, Harrow had ceased to be a town outside London, but part of the continuous built-up districts of North West London. It is, however, still officially in the ancient county of Middlesex.

A home of one's own was everybody's ambition in the 1920s and '30s. Static prices, easier mortgages and fairly good wages in the London area, plus a pioneering desire to be one's own master, even if there was little left over for furnishings or motor cars. Clever publicity (particularly by the Metropolitan Railway with its own Country Estates Company) and the pages of the London evening papers enticed reluctant Londoners out to the fresh fields or rural Harrow: 'Why pay landlords 7/6 a week for a flat when you can live in a home of your own at Harrow for 7/-?' or 'Live in Metroland' which become the best-known slogan of all. Another advertisement referring to Rayners Lane declared 'The din and toil of the streets are exchanged for an aspect of spreading landscapes of trees and green fields, where no sound assails the ears save the singing of the birds'.

Rayners Lane was a typical example of the rapid growth of Harrow's suburbs in the 1930s. The wooden-platformed station sold 4,000 tickets in 1929, although this is a rather suspect figure as there were no houses near the station! By 1938, when a fine new station was opened, four million tickets were sold. The Metropolitan Railway purchased land here and began the development of the Harrow Garden Village Estate in 1929. In its issue of 5 July, the *Harrow Observer* recorded: 'A new township is to rise where from time immemorial there has been nothing but farms and fields. An army of labourers is at work on the new arterial road to North Harrow station'. Just one year later, the paper stated:

A short year ago Rayners Lane was the loneliest station on the line, today it is the centre of a brand new residential suburb, complete with shops, schools and inhabited by hundreds of city workers. How this wonderful transformation has come about is a tribute to modern methods of mechanical science and hard work. For a year an army of workers aided by huge mechanical diggers and other up-to-date devices, have been building roads by the mile no where in the whole perimeter of London has a more remarkable development taken place during the past year, than that at Rayners Lane, it repays a visit at short intervals to see it grow, the township is rising fast and there will be no occasion here to lament in the future any lack of townplanning.

South of the railway, estate developer and builders T. F. Nash worked on the vast Tithe Farm and Rayners Lane estate. This was one of the largest private estates developed around London at the time. The proud new owners of the three-bedroom semi-detached Tudor style houses (£595) had all the amenities of a town with long parades of shops, and from 1936, the Grosvenor cinema. The cinema later became part of the Odeon chain and has survived several threats of closure. It has now been superbly restored and is once again called the Grosvenor. Of course many people lamented the passing of the fields and farms and old estates. Others cared nothing for the past. 'Residing in suburbia adds a thrill and zest to life. It is an experience in having no traditions to live up to', wrote one new resident.

'The trees are down/An Odeon flashes fire/Where stood their villa by the murmuring fir' – so wrote Sir John Betjeman about the changes that were sweeping Metroland. Others liked the new life and all it held in prospect. This is what a home-seeker wrote about arriving at North Harrow station in 1929:

> The immediate neighbourhood of the station appears to be taken up with builders' offices and builders' carts and lorries ... and more mud. The winter sunshine glinted on the bright red roofs of the little white houses – and in the distance trees, whose bare branches threaded delicate tracery against the clear blue sky.

Stained glass windows in the hall and on the landing. An 'Ideal' boiler, free electric light fittings, space for a garage – and a parade of convenient shops in addition to good bus and train services. This was a new and exciting life in a new and exciting Harrow.

> 'Ewbake'd inside and At'coed out ... the sunlight coming through the bottle glass of the front door falls in irregular blotches on the coconut mat made by ex-servicemen; on the fumed oak hat-stand and on the wall rack holding a library of walking sticks collected on summer holidays ... the blotches of light make the narrow hall seem rather dark by contrast. It smells faintly of furniture polish and somewhat more faintly of the American cloth of which the hood of a folding perambulator is made ... a perambulator for which there is really not enough room in the hall.'
>
> J. M. Richards *Castles on the Ground*, 1973

T. F. Nash, Cutler, A. Robinson, John Laing, Ideal Estates (John Searcy), H. Pickrill, Comben and Wakeling, E. S. Reid, The Artesian and General Property Co., J. Clare, A. J. King, F. and C. Costin (not to be confused with Costain) – these were just some of the hundreds of builders and developers great and small who transformed Harrow into the vast suburb it is today.

This was the age of the cinemas: small, medium, and super size like the Granada on the site of the old Greenhill Manor House, and the Dominion, down in Station Road. On the night of 4 June 1936 hundreds of people turned up to the opening of the cinema by Sir Isidore Salmon M.P. The audience were entertained by the music of the Joseph Mescani Orchestra, whilst B.B.C. impressionist Beryl Orde and America's greatest music and dancing act: Russell, Marconi and Vernon provided the cabaret. The film shown was *Our Little Girl* starring Shirley Temple; a popular tear-jerker, sure to please the suburban audience.

The shops of Greenhill were very popular at this time with Sopers department store (now Debenhams) where one could have afternoon tea whilst a trio played; or participate in social events amid the palms of Wright Cooper's Gayton Rooms. The shops along the Broadway or Station Road towards the Hill were superior to those in St Anne's Road. Here was a mixture of useful shops selling second-hand books, cycles, photographic equipment, furniture (from Adams Brothers) as well as sensible fashion and elegant hats for ladies at Somertons. The large villas of Lyon and Gayton Roads still brooded behind laurel hedges – an area where music teachers taught the piano to pupils who attended the many private schools. Older readers will remember Wealdstone in the 1930s where shopping came much cheaper. Hurford's the printers, Barnard's, Wooster's and the Poplar Stores. In High Street, street musicians could be heard (they were seldom in Station Road at Greenhill). The author can remember as a child seeing the old accordion player who always seemed to be in Wealdstone in all weathers. But of course, every district had its own particular characteristics: Wealdstone with the old Bridge Street Schools, the bright new parades of shops at Belmont, the wide pavements of Kenton with its rebuilt *Rest Hotel*. Select Woodcock Hill, Kenton station, Warner's the florists, Raymond's the drapers, the Express Dairy shop, the Odeon Cinema and the coal order office on the approach up to the station with its gigantic lump of coal let in the pavement outside; golf at Northwick Park and the single deck bus that took one to Kenton Lane, Christchurch Avenue and on to Wealdstone. Roxeth and South Harrow, where for years there was the prevailing smell of gas from the gas works, older shops that survived from Edwardian days, or Northolt Road, where semi-detached houses had been converted into shops – and yet another Odeon cinema.

By the 1960s Harrow began to change. Office blocks were erected in the town centre and the 1980s saw even more radical changes with the building of the St Anne's Centre and offices. Many old Greenhill landmarks slipped away. But Harrow is still essentially Metroland, and despite critics, suburbia is still the most popular place for a family to live.

> It appears to me that suburbs grew up to meet a definite economic need and, therefore, and that, therefore is a fact which some people may deplore, others applaud, but for whom it is difficult to find an alternative ... and for which the people who live in it have cause to be grateful.
>
> J. B. Priestley

Today, Harrow Hill still stands above green fields – but only a thin girdle around its feet. The once rolling cornfields and meadow are now a sea of red roofs, punctuated here and there with rocky islands of office blocks and flats. Harrow centre is showing all the warning signs of inner 'city' decay and it has lost some of its reputation as a major shopping centre. Yet, conversely, Harrow's suburbs have not changed a great deal. Its neat rows of semi-detached or detached houses still retain their bright front gardens. The roads are still tree-lined and Harrow has given a warm welcome over the last 25 years to people from many lands, races, and religions.

1. This is an 1816 view of Harrow's famous landmark, St Mary's church which dates from Norman times. The 200 ft.-spire was added *c.*1450: 'Low at her feet the rolling shire/Groves around her in green attire/And soaring above her, a silent spire/... Harrow-on-the-Hill.' *Harrow* by E. W. Howson

2. Church Fields and the famous tower and spire pictured in 1928. Charles Lamb walked through these fields and wrote about the 'instantaneous coolness and calming, almost transforming process of a country church' when he visited St Mary's.

3. The church was restored by Sir Gilbert Scott in 1846 and a facing of flints was put over the older walls. Near the porch is the recently-marked grave of Allegra, Byron's daughter (by Claire Claremount). She had a short but happy life from 1817 until 1822. Byron asked that she should be brought back from Switzerland to be buried in the churchyard that he had loved so well as a youth. Shelley wrote of her that: 'A lovelier toy sweet nature never made/A serious, subtle, wild, yet gentle being/Graceful, without design and unforeseeing.'

4. Interior of St Mary's church. In the restoration of 1846/9, Sir George Gilbert Scott removed the old galleries on the left-hand side. Further internal restoration took place in 1895 just before this view was taken. The pulpit seen here dates from 1675 although it was only given to the church in 1708.

5. The Vicarage and Lych Gate in 1900. The gate is in memory of the Rev. John Cunningham (Vicar from 1811-1861). During his time at the School, worship transferred from the church to the new Chapel in 1838 and Cunningham disapproved, fearing that the boys would be lost 'to Papacy'.

6. The Peachey tomb; the spot where Byron spent many hours in his youth. The protective iron grill was added in the middle of the 19th century to deter souvenir hunters. Byron wrote to his publisher, John Murray, on 26 May 1822: 'There is a spot in the churchyard, near the footpath, on the brow of the hill, looking towards Windsor, and a tomb under a large tree (bearing the name of Peachie or Peachey) where I used to sit for hours and hours when I was a boy.'

7. A visitor reads the plaque on the 'Byron' tomb. The famous elm mentioned by Byron seen here, was destroyed by a fire during the First World War.

8. A view taken *c.*1924 from St Mary's tower looking north east towards Kenton, Woodcock Hill and Stanmore.

9. Looking west in the 1920s, showing The Vaughan Library and the Butler Museum (the latter by Basil Champneys, 1886). The open fields towards North Harrow and Pinner have not yet been developed for housing estates. This photograph was taken from an aircraft.

10. The School Chapel was designed in 1855 by Sir Giles Gilbert Scott and was completed in 1857 with the addition of the spire in 1865. The building was said to have given 'increased freshness and beauty to the landscape'.

11. Going to Chapel, *c*.1913. The building hidden behind the ivy is Armstrong House, one of the two original school boarding houses.

12. Interior of the School Chapel, *c.*1923. The South Aisle (right) was added in 1856 in memory of Harrovians who fell in the Crimean War.

13. The Vaughan Library. The architect was Sir Giles Gilbert Scott. Lord Palmerston laid the foundation stone on a very wet July day in 1861.

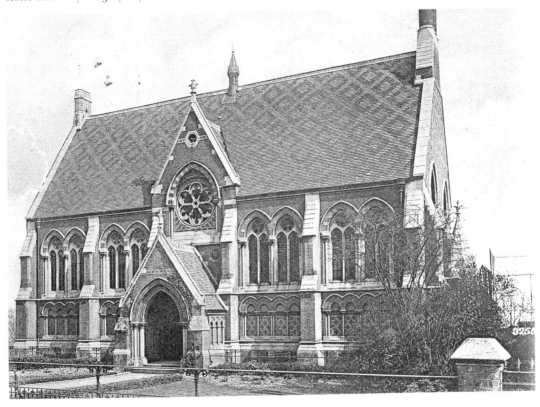

14. Calling the Bill or roll call in the yard outside the Old Schools: 'The buoyant boys, the clanging bell,/The whistling wind upon the Hill,/Dear Harrow, I have loved thee well.' W. E. Hine. The original School building is on the left, the right-hand side was added in 1819-20 by C. R. Cockerell who also designed the oriel windows.

15. Another view of the Old Schools. The ivy-covered house just behind the figures on the right is Armstrongs, a school boarding house founded by Robert Sumner, Headmaster 1760-71. It was demolished after the First World War to make way for the Memorial Building.

16. A fine view in the 1930s of the Old Schools, the Memorial Building, Speech Room and the Chapel.

17. After the First World War, the magnificent Memorial Building and steps were built. The architect was Sir Herbert Barker and the names of Harrovians who perished in both wars are listed on the walls under the arches. The words 'O Valiant hearts, who to your glory came' are inscribed on the walls.

18. The Speech Room was opened in 1877 to commemorate, rather belatedly, the tercentenary of the School celebrated in 1871 and the architect was the controversial William Burges of Cardiff Castle fame. Lord Aberdeen laid the foundation stone in 1874. The School had to wait until after the First World War before the towers were completed.

19. William Burges' designs for the interior of his Speech Room were so elaborate that they distressed the School Governors, and were revised several times before being accepted. This photograph shows the interior of the Speech Room in 1907.

20. A charming sketch showing the Speech Room and Art School. On the exterior wall of the Speech Room, by the road, is a plaque which apparently marks the site of a well where Charles I watered his horse and took his last view of London as a free man.

21. The Art School at the top of Grove Hill. W. Marshall was the architect (1896). On the right is Rendalls, a school boarding house, built in 1854.

22. The original Headmaster's house, the First Master's House, as it was in 1816. A disastrous fire almost completely destroyed the building on 22 October 1838. It was an event that caused a sensation in the sleepy Harrow area.

23. The present Headmaster's House in about 1902. It is in the style which Pevsner described when surveying the Harrow buildings as 'a hearty confident gloom'.

24. The town pump at the top of West Street. For centuries this was one of the local water supplies until the Harrow Water Company was founded in 1855. Water was sold at this pump for a halfpenny per pail. The pump was replaced by a fountain in 1880. Goshawk's Photographic Studio is the building behind.

25. West Street is one of the oldest side-roads on the Hill with the first record of it dating from 1453. A century ago it had nearly thirty shops. The half-timbered building seen in this drawing of the 1940s dates from 1557.

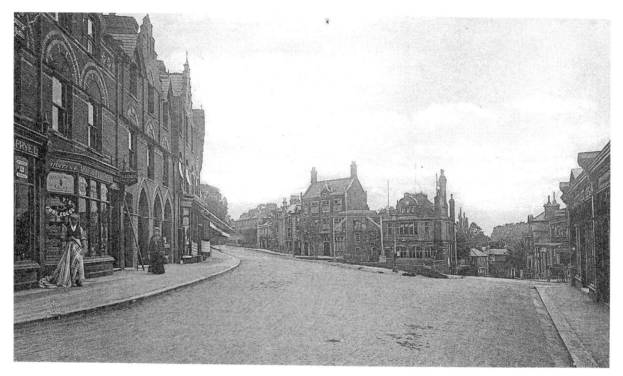

26. The centre of old Harrow-on-the-Hill with the old council Offices and fire station (1913) in the middle and the offices of the London and County Bank (now merged with the National Westminster). The Council offices were designed by C. W. Hayward in 1888. On the left is Frye's the grocery shop (later the International Stores) and the arches of the old Harrow post office (1878).

27. The *King's Head* and town green, 1903. Although founded in 1535 (according to the sign outside), the *King's Head* is mainly 18th-century with 19th-century additions. It was the departure point for local coaches, and later motor buses, to London, Harrow Weald and Watford. The building next to the inn with the shop on the ground floor is Harrow House. On the far right is the Public Hall designed by C. W. Hayward (1874). It later became the Elite cinema, one of the earliest picture palaces in the town.

28. High Street a century ago. The wall on the right is the boundary of The Park. Hartley the Chemist, in the middle of the picture, was owned by E. Hartley during the 1890s, who advertised 'Hartley's Silver Arrow Bouquet ... a delicate, refreshing and permanent perfume ... in bottles 1s 6d or 2s 6d' which could be sent anywhere post-free. The offices of the old *Harrow Gazette*, a local newspaper founded by William Winkley in 1855, are on the far left. The *Gazette* later merged with the *Harrow Observer*.

29. High Street near the junction with West Street in 1906. The house on the right is Flambards, one of the School houses. It stands near the site of a former manor house which was the home of Sir Edmund Flambard and his wife. They are commemorated by 14th-century brasses in St Mary's church.

30. High Street shortly after the Second World War, with the popular Ann's Pantry tea-rooms. The straw hats worn by the Harrow boys were apparently introduced by R. Blake, a local hatter in the 19th century.

31. Royal Visit, Speech Day, 30 June 1905.

32. 'As we welcomed the father so we welcome the son.' A rather odd banner supported by fire ladders from the nearby fire station erected for the visit of George V and Queen Mary on Speech Day, Saturday 15 June 1912. The *Harrow Observer* included in their report the improvements carried out at Wealdstone station: 'Not only do the King and Queen pay their first visit to the famous school on the hill, but the Willesden to Harrow section of the London and North Western Railway's new railway (the suburban line to Watford) will be opened, marking the first stage of a remarkable series of improvements.'

33. Grove Hill was the old road from the Hill to Greenhill and Harrow Weald until it was replaced by the less steeply-graded Peterborough Hill in the late 19th century. The trees on the left are in The Grove estate, which was a property of the Northwick family during the late 18th century.

34. Stately villas like those shown here became increasingly popular in the later years of the last century and in Edwardian times. On 25 February 1899 the junction here with Lowlands Road was the scene of what is said to have been Britain's first fatal car accident. The vehicle involved was a Daimler Wagonette. The driver, Edwin Sewell, had been recommended to the hirers-managers of the Army and Navy stores in Westminster as 'a splendid driver – a thoroughly reliable man', as indeed he was. Despite his skill, the technology of the time was unreliable, and one of the car's wheels broke up whilst descending Grove Hill. Sewell was killed instantly and one of his passengers died later.

35. Peterborough Hill near the junction with Kenton Road in 1936. Peterborough Road was constructed in 1879 and named after Dr. Butler, headmaster of Harrow (1805-29) who later became the Dean of Peterborough. The church tower is that of the old Baptist church in College Road.

36. The Ducker, Harrow School swimming pool, remained in use until modern times. The Ducker was in use from 1809 and in 1812 it was described as a rather muddy natural pond, with frogs and fish. Extensive improvements were made, particularly in 1881 when proper changing facilities were built. A caretaker's cottage was added in 1896.

37. Cricket had superseded archery as the main Harrow School sport by the beginning of the 19th century, and Byron is recorded as having played in a match against Eton. The pavilion seen here was built in 1885 from the designs of W. C. Marshall.

38. A tranquil view of the old Watford Road before 1914.

39. Near the same spot in 1938, with much house-building activity. The bus is on Route 18.

40. The old District Railway station at Sudbury Hill which opened in 1904. There were still open fields when this view was taken in 1929.

41. Sudbury Hill District Railway station (left) and Greenford Road looking towards Harrow Hill. At the bend is the bridge and the entrance to Sudbury Hill (Harrow) station of the Great Central Railway from Marylebone.

42. Harrow-on-the-Hill station and Lowlands in the early 1920s. To the left is Lowlands, the house and school buildings, with Lowlands Recreation Ground. Lowlands was the estate of Benjamin Rotch from 1829. He died in 1859 and his widow, Isabella, lived on there until 1909 when she died at the age of 100 years. She lived to see half the landscaped gardens sold to the Metropolitan Railway and witnessed the streets of Greenhill expand around her. In the 1830s, Lowlands was described as being in 'a very picturesque situation' and had a lawn with dappled deer. College Road in the 1920s still had its villas but already parades of shops can be seen. The house set amid the dense trees on the right of the railway is Hawarden Villa (now demolished, and the site is incorporated into the post office complex). The Baptist church is to be seen on the far right. The chimney of the Greenhill Laundry Company, St Anne's Road can be seen top right.

43. Lowland's Road at the junction of Station Approach (left) and Roxborough Park about 1905. The wooded Lowlands Estate is just by the figure of the lady.

44. Harrow-on-the-Hill station, *c*.1910. The station, which opened in 1880, was enlarged to accommodate the trains of the Great Central Railway (Marylebone opened in 1899) and the new electric services to Uxbridge which began in 1905, a year after the opening of the branch line.

45. *(above)* Waiting for the train at Harrow-on-the-Hill Met. station in 1933. The tower of the old Baptist church in College Road can be seen above the trees. The large posters in front of the post office sorting building are advertising Constance Bennett in *Sealed Lips* plus supporting acts at the new Embassy Cinema in North Harrow. There is also an advertisement for Lidstone, the butcher's, whose shop stood for many years at the junction of St Anne's Road and Station Road.

46. *(below)* Lowlands Road entrance to the station was the main approach for many years. This is a view taken *c.*1935 when plans were already being formulated for a new station. There was a fine set of iron gates where the approach joined Lowlands Road.

47. From 1905 to 1924, Aylesbury Metropolitan electric trains had to change to steam at Harrow for the onward journey to the Chilterns. This is the siding at Harrow station. The steam engine is an E class built at Neasden in 1896 and withdrawn in 1935.

48. Rare view of Uxbridge to Harrow steam shuttle train at Harrow-on-the-Hill, 1904. The branch line to Uxbridge was built in 1904 for electric traction, but electric trains did not begin running from Baker Street until January 1905.

49. The Girls' County School (now Greenhill College), Lowlands Road, 1922. The School opened shortly before the First World War and an advertisement published in 1914 announced 'The Girls' Grammar School – ventilation and sanitary arrangements are excellent; the whole building is warmed throughout and is lighted by electricity'.

50. Roxborough Park by the junction with Roxborough Avenue, March 1906. On the right is the Catholic church of St Thomas of Canterbury (dedicated 1894).

51. Roxborough Park was laid out with various styles of houses to suit City business men after the arrival of the Metropolitan Railway in 1880. The road was originally a trackway called Roxborough Lane which led to a farm.

52. Station Road with Bank Buildings, and the junction with College Road in the distance. The cycle delivery cart is outside the Home and Colonial stores. Boots the Chemist was still here until the late 1980s when the shop moved into the new St Anne's Centre. The trees are in front of the site of the Coliseum cinema.

53. A view of the famous Greenhill landmark in Station Road, the Coliseum cinema, which has now gone. The cinema was opened by Harrow's M.P., Oswald Mosley, on 11 October 1920. The films shown that day were *Alf's Button* and *Heart of Hills*. It brought luxury entertainment to Harrow with 2,000 seats priced from 1s.3d. to 3s.6d. The decor included blue carpets and curtains and buff, blue and gold walls and ceilings and was reviewed as 'The finest and best equipped cinema in Middlesex'. According to a contemporary advertisement, patrons could refresh themselves at 'an American style soda fountain'.

54. The twin towers of the old Coliseum were an essential part of Harrow for many years. The cinema was converted at the very end of the 1930s by Alfred Denville into a theatre for plays, music and ballet. It was a particularly popular dance place in the war years and for a decade afterwards. Joan Hammond, Heddle Nash, Sir Donald Wolfitt and Wilfred Pickles are a few of the famous names in music, drama and variety who appeared here. The theatre closed in July 1959 and was replaced by a supermarket.

55. We will turn off Station Road for a moment and walk down memory lane in College Road. This view dates from 1920, when the street was still partly residential. The Metropolitan and Great Central Railway station entrance can be seen on the right. On the left are the grounds of Heathfield School, orginally Harrow Day and Boarding School for Girls on Byron Hill Road. In 1901 the school moved to College Road and changed its name to Heathfield. At that time the headmistress was Miss Gayford. In the mid-1980s the school moved to Eastcote in order to make way for the St Anne's Centre.

56. College Road in the 1930s with an ST type bus on route 140. The tower belongs to the Baptist church which opened in 1908.

57. College Road, with a Green Line coach ('T' type) on route 703 passing Somerton's Ladies Fashion Store by the junction with Clarendon Road. This picture dates from the early 1960s before route 703 was withdrawn from service from 3 November 1964. Note that some of the old villa properties still remained although by this time they had become commercial premises.

58. Roxborough bridge on 24 July 1908 during the Olympic Marathon, from Windsor to White City, with the American John Joseph just crossing the Metropolitan Railway bridge. He was declared the winner although the Italian, Durando, was first past the post. As Durando entered the last lap in the Stadium he fell several times and was helped to his feet, thus disqualifying him. However, Queen Alexandra later presented him with a special consolation cup.

59. Station Road showing the old Technical or Art School. The building was opened in 1902 as Harrow Technical School and the architect was A. J. Batchelor. The building was extended in 1907. The school was later known as Harrow Technical School of Art. It moved to Northwick Park in 1970.

60. This view of Station Road dates from just after the Second World War. On the left are the offices of the *Harrow Observer* and Gas Board (originally the Gas Light and Coke Company). To the far right, builders have moved into what had been the premises of The Broadway Lending Library – 'popular novels for hire at 1d. a week'. Commercial libraries such as this (there were others at North Harrow and at Rayners Lane) filled a need when public libraries in the new suburbs were rare. These libraries were, perhaps, the old fashioned equivalent of today's video libraries. Shops on the corner of St Anne's Road in the distance included Lidstone the butcher, who had his own slaughter house behind the parade before 1914. The shop continued in business until the 1950s.

61. Greenhill Parade and St Anne's Road, *c.*1903. The shops here were built in 1900 to serve the needs of the population inhabiting the newly-developed streets laid out in Greenhill.

62. St Anne's Road opposite what is now the St Anne's Centre, *c.*1912.

63. Greenhill school, *c.*1900. The schools in St Anne's Road were founded in 1859 'for the children of labouring and other poorer classes'. The schools were rebuilt in 1896. The gentleman seen here is almost certainly Thomas Corby who was Headmaster from 1896 until 1922. In the 1970s the school was demolished to make way for the St Anne's development of the mid-1980s.

64. The corner of St Anne's Road and Station Road, *c*.1910. The houses on the right subsequently had shops built in their front gardens. In the distance can be seen the trees in front of Greenhill Manor House.

65. A quiet Sunday morning in December in the early 1960s. Notice the Christmas trees on the canopy of Sopers department store on the left-hand side of Station Road. Lilley and Skinner's shoe shop along the parade was a branch of the business founded by William Skinner and Thomas Lilley, who owned the land there before the shops were built. At the far end of the street you can just see the Granada cinema, built in 1938 on the site of Greenhill Manor.

FRANK PETTIFER,
CHEMIST,

PHOTOGRAPHIC, DISPENSING, & HOMŒOPATHIC.

HARROW PHARMACY STORES,

6 BANK BUILDINGS, GREENHILL.

Telephone: No. 223 P.O., Harrow.

Telephone : No. 293 P.O. Harrow.   *The "Greenhill" House Furnishers.*

A. J. Thomson & Co., (Several years with Maple & Co. Ltd.)

24 GREENHILL PARADE, HARROW.

Cabinetmakers, Upholsterers, House Furnishers.

Casement Draw Blinds a Speciality.

French Polishing and General Fixing done.
Carpets taken up, Beaten, and Re-laid.
Removals by Road or Rail.
Artistic Draping.   Estimates Free.

Telephone : No. 152 P.O., Harrow.

A. S. Heffer,

Builder and Decorator,
Station Road, Harrow.

And at ...
The Bridge,
Wealdstone.   Estimates for Repairs
· · · · ·

WILLIAM COLE, Electrician,

20 GREENHILL PARADE, HARROW
(Opposite Greenhill Elementary Schools).

Electrical and Gas Lighting Sundries.
Electric Motors and Radiators. . . .

PLUMBING, GAS AND HOT WATER FITTING.

THE ...
Harrow Estate Offices.

— MESSRS. —

CLARKE & CO.

House and Estate Agents, ...
Auctioneers, Surveyors, and Architects,

PETERBOROUGH ROAD and HIGH STREET,

HARROW ; and at WEALDSTONE.

PRINTED REGISTER, with Map of the District,
FREE UPON APPLICATION.

Telephone: No. 219 P.O., Harrow.   Telegrams: "Hammer, Harrow."

ONE HUNDRED ELMS FARM,

SUDBURY, NEAR HARROW.

BRANCHES:

1 WEST ST., HARROW. | 121 HEADSTONE ROAD, HARROW. | 4 GREENHILL PARADE.

The most Modern and Sanitary Dairies in Harrow or Sudbury.

All Produce guaranteed Pure, Fresh, and of the Highest Quality at Lowest Prices.

STERILIZED AND HUMANIZED MILK.

The Inhabitants of Harrow, Greenhill, Sudbury, and Wembley are respectfully solicited
to call and inspect the Farm Cowsheds and Dairies. Samples and Price Lists sent
gratis on application to H. FLOREY, One Hundred Elms Farm, Sudbury, Middlesex.

For 'A PERFECT BREAD OF HEALTH,' eat

WRIGHT COOPER BROS.'

'ELECTRIC' MACHINE-MADE BREAD

(GOLD, SILVER, AND BRONZE MEDALS).

CONFECTIONERS and CATERERS,

HARROW-ON-THE-HILL.

Telephone : No. 121 P.O., Harrow.

---

67. Clarke and Co., Estate Agents were trading in Greenhill before the First World War and continued in business as late as the 1970s. Another Greenhill trader established before the First World War was Wright Cooper Bros. who opened at the Gayton Rooms and bakery along the parade towards Sopers. Wright Cooper had been a chef with the P and O steamship line before opening his first shop on the Hill. The Station Road shop opened in 1900 and closed in about 1959.

68. Lyon Road, *c*.1914. The influence of the architect Norman Shaw can be seen in these houses which echo Bedford Park at Turnham Green. Huge office blocks have now replaced nearly all the houses of Lyon Road and Gayton Road.

69. St John's church and the Victoria Hall, Greenhill. The church replaced an earlier Italianate-style church consecrated in December 1866. The present church dates from 1905, but was not finally completed for many years. Victoria Hall was opened in 1888 and enlarged in 1906 when it was in use as a private school. During the Second World War, and for a few years afterwards, it was a British Restaurant. Kenmare House once stood opposite, the site of which became Harrow's first department store, founded by W. H. Soper in 1914. Unfortunately, he died in the great flu epidemic of 1918 and the shop traded for some time as Green and Edwards, but reverted to Sopers in the 1920s. It grew to become one of the largest stores in north-west London. It has now been rebuilt and is a branch of Debenhams. The Victoria Hall was demolished in 1963.

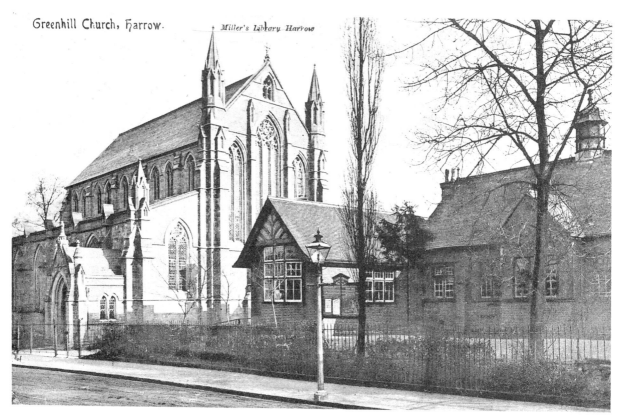

70. A rare picture of pupils in the grounds of St Margaret's school in Station Road, Greenhill. The school occupied the house and gardens of an old property called The Crofts which stood between Bonersfield Lane and Elmgrove Lane.

71. The owners of the St Margaret's school were the Neumann sisters and, when war broke out in 1914, they had to return to Germany. The school survived, however, and later moved to Sheepcote Road. The Crofts site was developed for shopping parades just before the Second World War.

72. Rutland Road in 1913 was a typical Edwardian street off the Pinner Road. Note the tradesmen's delivery vehicles in the distance.

73. Pinner View, a typical 'Metroland' street of the inter-war years in 1939. The first houses were built from about 1905 although various sites were not fully built up until modern times.

74. West Harrow station was opened in February 1914 at the request of the new local residents. This photograph dates from c.1934.

75. A view of Pinner Road dated 1906 in the days when it led to Hooking Green, the district that was later to be called North Harrow. The name dates back at least to 1754. The Yeading or Lankers Brook passed under the road here.

LOOKING FOR A HOUSE?
TRY HARROW

There are plenty of houses and frequent services
of through trains from Harrow-on-the-Hill, North
Harrow, South Harrow, West Harrow or Rayners
Lane Stations. List of estate agents and builders
and full particulars of season ticket rates from

LONDON TRANSPORT, 55, BROADWAY, S.W.1

VICtoria 6800

Increase your leisure by living on the

E1/600

76. A poster issued in 1934 at the height of the Metroland housing boom.

77. An 1868 drawing of Headstone Manor by Albert Hartshorn. The moated building with parts dating back at least to the 15th century is now being restored as part of Harrow Heritage Centre.

78. Headstone Manor and the 16th-century tithe barn which is now Harrow Heritage Centre. For centuries, Headstone was the property of the Archbishops of Canterbury, and the site is one of the most historic in the Harrow area.

79. The moat at Headstone Manor in 1900. The moat was probably an ornamental feature in the 14th century, stocked with fish and useful for keeping animals out of the farm garden. In Edwardian days, Headstone was known as Moat Farm. The moat is believed to be the only complete one of its kind in Middlesex.

80. Station Road, Wealdstone in 1902. It makes a peaceful contrast to the same scene today, although many of the houses seen here still remain. On the left stood Bridge schools, demolished in the 1970s to make way for the Civic Centre. Station Road was originally Greenhill Lane.

81. High Street, Wealdstone, with the old *Queen's Arms* in the 1890s. It was many years before building near the station began in earnest. One guide-book writer described the scene: 'Round the site finally chosen for the railway station, there sprang up, on either side of the ancient Harrow lane, a collection of mediocre houses and shops'.

82. The opening years of the 20th century saw more shops opening along High Street. This scene is by the junction with Masons Avenue. Arthur Flint ran the drapery stores. On the extreme right, R. E. Bunting's cycle shop is under construction. Remarkably, the same business is still there today, almost the last to survive, along with Woosters the coal merchants across by the station, of the pre-War Wealdstone shops.

83. High Street, *c.*1899. Note the new shops under construction near the junction with Grant Road.

84. Coronation Parade, 1911, looking towards the junction with Headstone Drive and Holy Trinity church. The steeple of the old Mission Hall (later the Red Triangle Club of the Y.M.C.A.) can be seen in the centre distance with the Magistrate's Court, built 1909, to the left.

85. Holy Trinity church. The foundation stone was laid in August 1880 and the church was consecrated in June 1881.

86. Headstone Drive and Holy Trinity church looking towards High Street, *c.*1914.

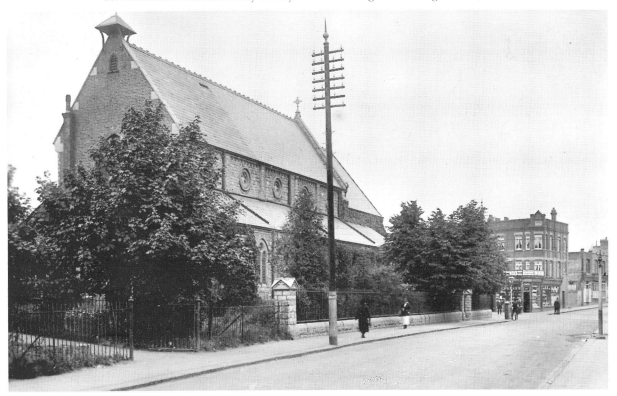

87. A Mothers' Union outing about to depart, with everyone dressed in best clothes, outside Holy Trinity church, *c.*1909. The vehicles were hired from J. Knott, carriage builder, of High Street.

88. High Street *c.*1902 with the *Duke of Edinburgh* public house on the right, and the lamp-post outside the old fire station. The fire engine was actually kept in the premises of J. Knott, the local carriage builder, until a new station opened in Palmerston Road in 1906.

89. Delivery service in High Street *c.*1896.

90. High Street in Edwardian days. This parade of shops was built in 1899. The shop on the corner is now a supermarket.

91. Wealdstone Baptist chapel was opened in October 1905. The building adjacent to the chapel is the Wealdstone Hall.

BAPTIST CHAPEL AND HIGH STREET, WEALDSTONE.

92. High Street just after the Second World War, with an STL lowdeck bus designed to pass under low bridges. Note the headquarters of the Harrow Communist Party and the advertisement for the *Daily Worker* newspaper in the window.

93. *The Case is Altered*, High Street, with Garraway's Cab yard, which had been acquired by S. Trewin by the time that this picture was taken *c.*1912.

94. The Memorial Clock Tower which was unveiled by Lt. General Ironside on 11 November 1923. The house behind the tower was called Ravenscroft and was the practice of Dr. Butler, local medical officer for health. It was pulled down in the 1960s and replaced with flats.

95. A view taken shortly before the Second World War. The Memorial was damaged on 23 August 1940 in one of the very first air raids over Harrow. Along the street to the left can be seen the rather austere architecture of the Hergra Cinema, now a retail store for electrical goods.

96. High Road at the junction with Clairmont Road. The house on the right is now the *Clairmont Hotel*. Ladysmith Road is on the left.

97. Rural Wealdstone at the beginning of the century showing the footpath over the fields at Belmont. The name was originally spelt 'Belmount' after the shape of the hill here.

98. The new station buildings designed by Gerald Horsley for the improvement schemes carried out by the L.N.W.R. between 1911-12. The bricks used for the building were specified as 'best hard, sound square well-burned stocks'. When the tragic Harrow train crash occurred in October 1952, the impact as the trains collided was so forceful that the clock stopped at nineteen minutes and thirty seconds past eight in the morning. (The actual crash was a minute before but the clock was always a minute fast.) This picture dates from about 1919. Note the poster on the right advertising a 'Heroes Dinner' for returning servicemen.

99. The old main entrance to the station, originally called Harrow, which was renamed Harrow and Wealdstone on 1 August 1897. This 1912 picture shows two L.N.W.R. Leyland buses. The one nearest the camera is bound for Watford (a route which began in 1906 via Harrow Weald and Bushey) and the other vehicle is for Greenhill and the shopping centre.

100. The L.N.W.R. express is shown near Headstone Lane station. The new electric tracks of the L.N.W.R. and Bakerloo lines are to be seen in the foreground. Headstone Lane station was opened in February 1913.

101. New buildings for the Eastman Dry Plate Company at Headstone Drive about 1901. Kodak acquired the site in 1890, because it was felt that the clear air of the countryside would be highly beneficial for the manufacture of photographic materials. There is also a legend that local cattle would be the source of the gelatine for use in the processing. The company began operations in 1891 and remains the principal employer in the Harrow area. On the top of the building to the right is the original Kodak advertising slogan: 'You press the button, we do the rest'. The company originally had five artesian wells on the site.

102. Under the bridge: Headstone Drive with R.L.H. type bus on route 230 (North Park to Rayners Lane via Kenton and Wealdstone). This was a special 'low' double decker for negotiating routes with reduced height bridges. Sopers' advertisement mentions amongst its facilities a food department and restaurant.

103. London Transport was very short of buses in the late 1940s and new vehicles intended for provincial companies were sent to operate some routes. This photograph of 1950 shows a Bristol type bus at the stop outside the Kodak factory.

104. An interesting view of Roxeth taken *c.*1920. Northolt Road is prominent, running from top to bottom of the picture. The District Railway's old station is far right with the viaduct crossing what was once Roxeth Marsh towards Rayners Lane. The Gas Works, founded in September 1855, pre-dated the railway with carts transporting the coal from Wealdstone.

105. Roxeth church, designed by Sir Gilbert Scott, was consecrated in 1862. From 1877 until 1907 the Rev. John Floyd Andrews was the vicar here; a distinctive figure walking around his parish in a long old-fashioned cassock and 'shovel'-type hat. He had the vestry built and the floor of the church decorated in mosaic.

106. Building the Metropolitan Railway viaduct across Roxeth Marsh in 1903. The contractor was Bott and Stannett and this is one of their light steam locomotives (an 0-6-0ST called Gordon) which was used to bring supplies on temporary tracks. On completion, the viaduct was praised as 'a fine specimen of engineering skill'. Oddly enough, passenger trains (operated by the District Railway) did not use the connection from South Harrow station to Rayners Lane until 1910 due to legal difficulties.

107. Living rough; one of the colourful navvies who built the Roxeth Viaduct beside his temporary turf 'home' in the summer of 1903.

108. Old South Harrow station building
in 1933 with ST type buses on route
114. Later this route was extended to
the new suburb of Rayners Lane. The
new station site was by Northolt Road
bridge and opened on 5 July 1935.

109. The District Railway station
opened on 28 June 1903 as 'SOUTH
HARROW for Roxeth and Northolt'.

110. Old South Harrow station with District and Piccadilly Line trains in 1932. The banner reads 'Through express trains to the West End and Finsbury Park'. This was prior to the extension northwards to Arnos Grove and, later, Cockfosters. Piccadilly tube trains replaced District trains to Uxbridge via Rayners Lane from October 1933.

111. Flook's miniature atlantic railway at the Paddocks which operated during holidays and when there were sufficient visitors. Apparently the usual operating days were Thursdays and Saturdays in July and August between 1912-14. Later, part of the grounds were incorporated into Alexander Park in what is now called South Harrow.

112. A day at the Paddocks, *c*.1912. Children enjoy an excursion to rural Roxeth. This was photographed in Northolt Road near Park Lane.

113. For many years the Paddocks was a popular venue for Sunday School treats and children's outings. This picture shows the gardens around the Paddocks Farm House. As many as 3,000 visitors could be accommodated on busy days. The gardens were run by Mr. A. B. Champniss. Some of the buildings seen here were originally used by the contractor during the construction of the Metropolitan Railway at Rayners Lane.

114. Alexandra Avenue near the junction with Eastcote Lane *c*.1932 when the new South Harrow was being built. The new road runs across Newton Field towards the slight rise of ground at Rayners Lane. On the left edge of the view is a haystack at Tithe Farm. The lands were purchased from Christ Church Oxford on 15 June 1931 for £64,895 and developed by T. F. Nash, the largest of the pre-War builders of suburban Harrow. One of the last tenant farmers to live at the old farmhouse was Alfred Priest, who died in 1916 and was buried at Roxeth. The farm was eventually replaced by the *Tithe Farm Hotel*.

115. Advertisement from the *Evening Standard*, December 1933, for houses on Nash's South Harrow estate. By this date Piccadilly Line tube trains had replaced the old District Railway and had commenced running through to Rayners Lane and on to Uxbridge.

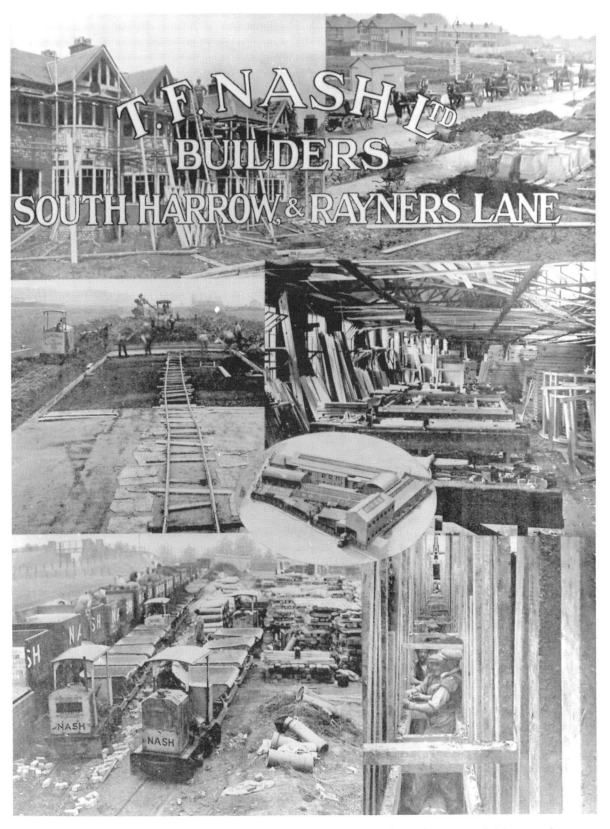

116. Advertisement for T. F. Nash estates, *c.*1934. The centre right picture shows the company's joinery works at Wealdstone. Bottom left are the sidings at High Worple, Rayners Lane, with the transfer to narrow gauge railway for the vast estate being built south of the station.

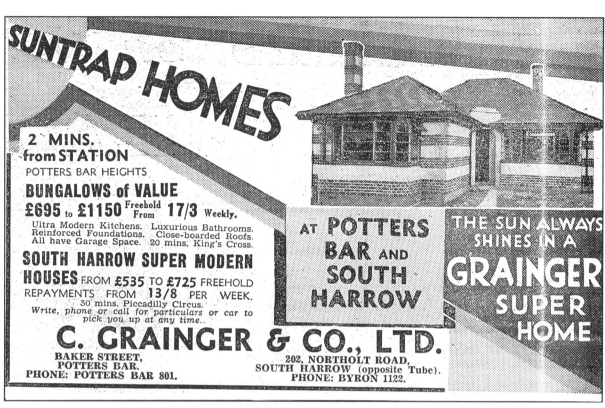

117. Grainger's sun-trap homes – an advertisement from *The Evening News*, 1936.

118. The earliest known photograph of Rayners Lane. In this 1903 photograph the new junction and railway bridge is under construction. The figure on the bridge is Walter Atkinson, engineer for Bott and Stannett, the contractors.

119. This view taken from Cannon Lane bridge shows railway-owned land being ploughed in the winter of 1915 as part of the Metropolitan's 'Dig for Victory' campaign. Village Way now runs across these fields.

120. A 1933 view looking towards Harrow from old Rayners Lane bridge. Soon after this photograph was taken the signal box was demolished by a run-away goods train. Harrow Hill can be seen in the background and considerable suburban development has already taken place.

121. Rayners Lane station opened on 25 May 1906. An early traveller on the line recalled some years ago that: 'One stood on the wooden platform in the early summer and the air was filled with the singing of countless larks, and the scent of hayfields'. In the winter, however, it could be a bleak place to wait for one of the infrequent trains on the District railway to South Harrow and the station was known as 'pneumonia junction'.

TYPICAL ROBINSON-BUILT RESIDENCES, HIGH WORPLE,
HARROW GARDEN VILLAGE.

A HOUSE IN A HUNDRED

YES, a house in a hundred, and its true ! Planned to please ;
built to last and sold at prices that are definitely " rock
bottom " Robinson's " Quality " houses will instinctively
appeal to those in search of a superior house at reasonable
cost. They are soundly built in brick, skilfully planned,
excellently appointed and represent the successful outcome of
a keen endeavour to satisfy every need.

They are situated on the delightful Harrow Garden Village
Estate only twenty minutes from Town ; they are replete with
every convenience ; vary in type and plan, and range from
£875 to £1,150 freehold. A nominal deposit will readily secure
immediate possession, whilst a particularly accommodating
system of gradual payment renders their purchase even less
expensive than paying rent.

Come and see them for yourself at our expense—take a cheap
ticket at any Metro. station to Rayners Lane, adjoining Estate,
and our representative will promptly refund your outlay.

A.ROBINSON BUILDER
HARROW GARDEN VILLAGE
ADJOINING RAYNER'S LANE STATION

122. In 1930 A. Robinson built some of the first houses south of the railway in High Worple and Worple
Way.

123. Nash employed nearly 1,000 workers and the company had its own joinery works at Wealdstone. Notice in this view of houses under construction at Rayners Lane in 1934 that horse-drawn transport is still being used. 'Travelling for only half an hour or so from London, you will find an estate still retaining the unmarred beauties and the unspoiled healthy atmosphere of Nature in all her most beautiful aspects.'

124. This is a typical advertisement from the *Evening Standard*, 1935. The largest development at Rayners Lane was that of T. F. Nash Limited. They advertised extensively in the London evening newspapers: 'From Piccadilly to the Pic' of the houses in less time than it takes to read the evening paper'.

125. Line up of saloon cars used to transport prospective buyers from Rayners Lane and South Harrow stations to view plots on the Nash estates, which were so large that many sites were a good mile or more from the station; a fact which buyers only discovered when they moved to their new homes!

126. The arch over Alexandra Avenue (named after Princess Alexandra) in July 1934 designed for a local Grand Shopping Week. Old Rayners Lane station can be seen in the distance. Ceremonial firework displays were also a popular method of selling new estates, and both Nash and E. S. Reid held Gala Bonfire Nights. One held on the Harrow Garden Village estate was said to have had the largest bonfire ever seen in Harrow's long history. By the end of the 1930s, the old Harrow, high on its hill, was left a green island amid an ocean of red-brick houses and arterial roads.

127. This is the recently restored Grosvenor cinema in Alexandra Avenue which was designed by Andrew Mather and opened in October 1936. The cinema was re-named the Odeon in 1937. Attractions included 'two live West End variety acts on Saturday nights' and a tea room, with Lloyd Loom chairs and glass topped tables, and a 'Hollywood style ladies' cosmetic room for lady patrons' – no doubt to allow the discrete repair of tear-stained make-up after the latest Clark Gable film.

128. An advertisement of 1937 for houses alongside the Piccadilly Line at Rayners Lane on the Cliffords estate. Note the offer 'Special terms to Civil Servants, bank officials etc.'.

DO YOU WANT TO BE NEAR A STATION?

If so, see the "BYRON HOUSES" within 3 minutes of Rayners Lane Station, which is on the Metro Line and Piccadilly Tube and District Railways. Access to any part of Town. Trains every few minutes. Low Season rates. Baker Street in under 30 minutes.

Well-built Tudor and ultra-modern designs to give very large rooms, beautifully fitted. 3 bedrooms, bathroom, separate W.C., 2 sitting rooms and big modernised kitchen. Garage space and large garden.

£695
FREEHOLD INCLUDING ALL COSTS AND CHARGES.

17/1 WEEKLY.

LOW DEPOSIT TO SUIT. SPECIAL TERMS TO CIVIL SERVANTS, BANK OFFICIALS, ETC.

CLIFFORDS RAYNERS LANE ESTATE, HARROW.

TURN RIGHT AND FIRST LEFT FROM RAYNERS LANE STATION.

Illustrated details sent post free on request from
CLIFFORD'S ESTATES, 225, Northolt Road, South Harrow. 'Phone Byron 2921.

129. Alexandra Avenue, Rayners Lane c.1960 with Nash shopping parade on the right. Note the United Dairies shop – familiar sight in most London suburban parades at this time.

The Old Church, Stanmore.

130. Stanmore Old church was built by Sir John Woolstanholme in 1632 to replace the original decayed ancient building.

131. An early photograph of Great Stanmore 'new' church. George Hamilton Gordon, 4th Earl of Aberdeen, provided £2,000 towards the building fund. His son, Douglas, was Rector at the time.

132. St John's church, Great Stanmore, 1910. The foundation stone was laid on 14 March 1849 by Lord Aberdeen in the presence of Queen Adelaide, widow of William IV. It was her last public engagement, as she died a short time afterwards at her home in Bentley Priory. The ivy-covered ruined tower of the original church is visible just above the lych gate.

133. The grave of W. S. Gilbert (1836-1911). He spent the later years of his life at Grimsdyke House, Harrow Weald. The circumstances of his death are slightly obscure, but the most generally accepted story is that he died of a heart attack brought on when he dived into the lake on his estate to save a young girl from drowning.

134. A photograph of Church Road showing the old water pump, *c.*1900. The buildings behind were demolished in the early 1930s to make way for shops.

135. Little Common, Stanmore; still a rural spot in the 1960s.

136. The pond at Stanmore Common, 1903. It is still recognisable today.

137. Peaceful days in the pre-1914 era. A 'B' type bus on route 142 waits on Stanmore Hill for the photographer.

138. Ginger's butchery on Stanmore Hill photographed during the late 19th century. The delivery trap was used to take meat to the great houses, such as Bentley Priory and Stanmore Park, twice daily.

139. The old post office, Stanmore Hill, 1907.

140. Corner of Stanmore Hill and The Broadway, *c.*1934. The village hall, known as the Berneys Institute, is along to the right. Modern shops now occupy the site of the cottage on the left.

141. The *Abercorn Arms*, Stanmore Hill, takes its name from the 18th-century owners of Bentley Priory. In 1935, when this picture was taken, motorists could stop for lunch (2s.6d.) or dinner (3s.6d.). It was here that the Watford to London coach stopped twice daily to change horses in the 1820s. The bus is an ST type from Watford to Kilburn.

142. London General Omnibus route 142 (previously route 102) at *The Vine* on the very top of Stanmore Hill. Bus excursions were popular along this road. Back in 1845, *The Vine* was a stopping place for the Bushey to London coach.

143. The Broadway, 1931. The village was already changing into a suburb and new parades of shops were being built in anticipation of the opening of the Metropolitan Railway's branch line from Wembley Park.

144. The special train at the opening of Stanmore's original station on Thursday 18 December 1890. The branch from Harrow and Wealdstone was operated by the L.N.W.R. The locomotive is a Webb 2-4-2 tank engine, a type used on this line for many years.

145. The Stanmore L.N.W.R. station was designed to blend with the nearby church. After closure in 1953, the building was much altered but still remains as a private house. The waggon seen here is a local delivery service for William Whiteley's department store, in Bayswater in London.

146. A train waiting to depart for Belmont and Harrow and Wealdstone in 1934. The station and its small freight yard retained a delightful rural atmosphere even when Stanmore became more urbanised. The passenger service was withdrawn in 1952 although trains were still used for freight until 1964.

147. Building the Metropolitan Railway to Stanmore. This is a Manning Wardle 0-6-0 saddle tank engine (possibly Watford-built in 1876) working on a temporary track in the countryside which was later to become the approach to the new terminus.

148. The same view as the previous picture, two years later in 1932. The new Metropolitan station is nearing completion. A fairly lavish goods yard was laid out, including cattle pens – a rather eccentric addition to a new branch of the underground.

149. Early days on the new Metropolitan Railway; a single car electric train near Canons Park on off-peak shuttle duty. The new branch provided extensive services with 144 trains each day. This view was taken 5 August 1934.

150. Constructing the railway bridge over Whitechurch Lane, Canons Park, 1931.

151. The new Canons Park (Edgware) station in December 1932, shortly after its opening. A poster on the station announces 'New Met. line to Baker Street, the City and West End'. The suffix 'Edgware' was discontinued after the formation of London Transport in 1933. The Metropolitan service was replaced by the Bakerloo Line from 20 November 1939 which was superseded by the Jubilee Line in 1979.

152. Harrow Weald Park, Brookshill, Harrow Weald, was built in 1805 and was the home of the Rev. J. W. Cunningham until 1822. The property was later purchased by Henry Crockford, of Crockford's famous gambling club, and he lived here until 1850. In the 1870s the house was owned by Alexander Sim, founder of the Colne Valley Water Company (1873). Between 1932-38 the property was occupied by the British-Israel World Federation. Harrow Council demolished the house some years ago and homes for the elderly now cover part of the site. Sections of the outbuildings and lodges survive along with the woods.

153. The 'City', Harrow Weald; a hamlet of cottages in Old Redding near the Harrow Weald public house called *The Case is Altered*. The name Weald comes from the old English word for forest and 'redding' – a forest clearing.

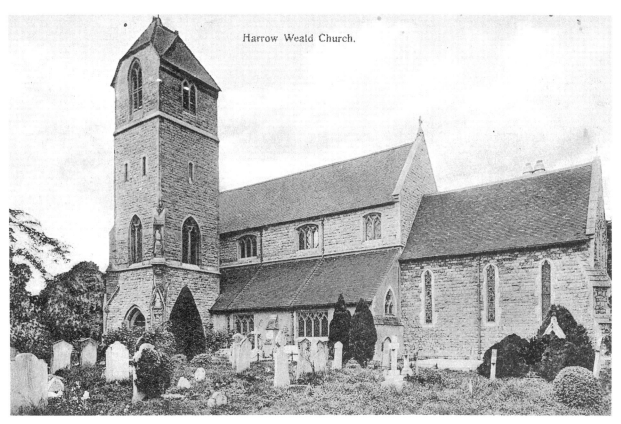

Harrow Weald Church.

154. All Saints' church, Harrow Weald was begun by J. T. Harrison in 1846, but the nave and south aisle were undertaken by William Butterfield in 1849. One of Butterfield's last works, the tower, was not added until 1890.

155. The Vicarage, Harrow Weald.

156. The Lych Gate at All Saints' church was an Edwardian memorial dedicated to the Rev. Edward Monro, author of 'Sacred Allegories'. He was vicar here for 20 years and was also founder of a training college for church schoolmasters.

157. Anthony's Farm, High Road, Harrow Weald, 1907. It was named after J. S. Anthony who ran a large dairy business. This is one of his carts by the old pond. The young Anthony Trollope once lodged here when he was a day pupil at Harrow School in 1830.

158. This view of The Rest tea-rooms dates from well before the First World War. When Kenton was being developed after 1919, The Rest was reconstructed as a smart suburban 'hotel' with many bars and saloons. Back in 1933, the then Proprietor of the new hotel, W. Silcock, advertised accommodation for '150 diners – lunch 2/6d'; at the rear beautiful gardens were recommended for tea in summer time. It is now known as *The Traveller's Rest*.

159. The Rest tea-rooms in the days when Kenton was described as 'a dreamy little hamlet set in a sea of emerald with a few old cottages'. The Rest was a popular place for outings, particularly after Kenton station opened on the L.N.W.R.'s 'New Line' to Watford in 1913.

THE NORTHWICK ESTATE

NORTHWICK PARK & KENTON

LONDON'S NEW SUBURB

9 miles from the Marble Arch.
14 minutes from Baker Street.
Served by three Electric Railways.
Over 100 Trains each way every day.

A UNIQUE SPECIMEN OF TOWN PLANNING

The Largest and best laid out Estate near London.

Delightful & Artistic Freehold Houses for Sale

Each a distinctive Ideal Home in every sense of the word.
Splendidly built, only the best material being used.
Perfect rural surroundings, Lovely views, Extraordinarily healthy.
Well constructed Roads. Main Drainage. Electric Light and Gas,
and Colne Valley Water.

WOODCOCK HILL LANE.

SAY YOU SAW IT IN "METRO-LAND."

106

160. The rebuilt *Rest Hotel* in 1935, showing the corner of Station Avenue which was one of the very first roads to be developed just before the First World War. It was renamed Carlton Avenue in the 1920s. When the L.N.W.R.'s 'New Lines' were opened, the Company issued a booklet called 'North-West Country Homes'. Prospective passengers and future home buyers were told that the new suburban railway was 'drawing new residents out from London to the pleasant places still to be occupied in the 17 miles between Euston and Watford. Cheap rents ... proper sanitation ... good schools ... excellent golf courses ... ample water supply' were some of the virtues of as yet undeveloped places such as Kenton.

161. An advertisement dating from 1929 for the Northwick Park estate. The Churchill-Rushout family developed their old lands at Harrow after the First World War and many of the roads were named after places near their estate; Northwick Park, Blockley near Moreton in Marsh.

162. The Aylesbury to Baker Street train passing through the Northwick Park estate in 1957. The electric locomotive is number 18 'Michael Faraday'.

163. This photograph was taken near Kenton before 1924 showing a L.N.W.R. express hauled by a Claughton Class engine. Note the recently laid down electrified tracks for Bakerloo and L.N.W.R. (L.M.S.) trains.

164. This is Kenton bridge and the L.M.S. (originally L.N.W.R.) station in April 1933. The station was served by L.M.S. electric trains and also tube trains of the Bakerloo Line. Next to the station exit is J. Warner's florist shop – a business very popular on Friday nights and Saturday lunchtimes when office workers (mainly male) returned home for the weekend, and wanted flowers for their wives. Note the prominent estate agent's board advertising new houses ranging from £595 to £2,000 with weekly repayments of 19s.1d. on the Edwards and H.R.P. estates.

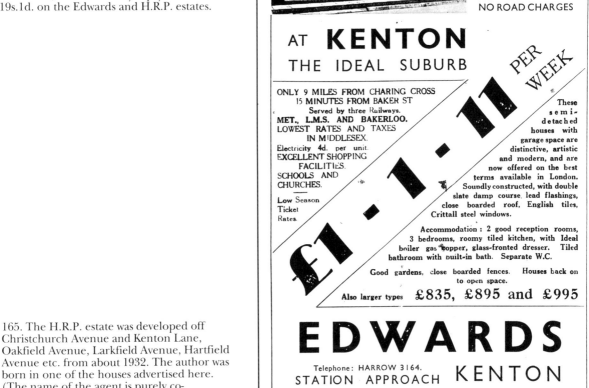

FREEHOLD
£785

Total Deposit
£50

NO LAW COSTS
NO ROAD CHARGES

AT **KENTON**
THE IDEAL SUBURB

£1 · 1 · 11 PER WEEK

ONLY 9 MILES FROM CHARING CROSS
15 MINUTES FROM BAKER ST
Served by three Railways.
MET., L.M.S. AND BAKERLOO.
LOWEST RATES AND TAXES
IN MIDDLESEX.

Electricity 4d. per unit.
EXCELLENT SHOPPING
FACILITIES.
SCHOOLS AND
CHURCHES.

Low Season
Ticket
Rates.

These semi-detached houses with garage space are distinctive, artistic and modern, and are now offered on the best terms available in London. Soundly constructed, with double slate damp course, lead flashings, close boarded roof, English tiles, Crittall steel windows.

Accommodation : 2 good reception rooms, 3 bedrooms, roomy tiled kitchen, with Ideal boiler gas copper, glass-fronted dresser. Tiled bathroom with built-in bath. Separate W.C.

Good gardens, close boarded fences. Houses back on to open space.

Also larger types £835, £895 and £995

EDWARDS
Telephone: HARROW 3164.
STATION APPROACH KENTON

165. The H.R.P. estate was developed off Christchurch Avenue and Kenton Lane, Oakfield Avenue, Larkfield Avenue, Hartfield Avenue etc. from about 1932. The author was born in one of the houses advertised here. (The name of the agent is purely co-incidental!)

166. Kenton Road in 1934. On the left at the corner of Carlton Avenue and by the *Rest Hotel* is Raymond's, the drapers. Other shops along this parade include J. Sainsbury and W. H. Smith. On the other side of the road is the North Met., the Electricity Showrooms and the Express Dairy shop. Further along the road on the left again was the Odeon cinema, which opened in 1935. It was pulled down in 1965 and the site is now occupied by a Waitrose supermarket. The bus route 183 through Kenton began in 1927.

167. 'Live on Kenton Hill' – an advertisement for the Woodcock Hill area of Kenton dating from 1932. The residents of Woodcock Hill and Northwick Park were offered excellent sports facilities – an essential selling point in those days of middle-class pretensions and 'lobelias and tennis flannels' (T. S. Eliot). The Palaestra sports ground was particularly popular.

168. Advertising F. and C. Costin housing in 1934 (not to be confused with the present-day large construction firm of Costain). Costin's houses were offered as being 'Vastly superior to anything offered at a higher price ... happily placed on Kenton's highest point (330ft. above sea level) where the air is invigorating and the climate dry'.

169. Costin's joinery works and yard at South Kenton, alongside the L.M.S. main line just south of the Metropolitan Railway bridge. Both motor-powered and horse-drawn transport is in evidence.

170. Kenton Recreation Ground at the end of Carlton Avenue beside the L.M.S main line – an ideal spot for youthful train spotters 60 years ago. The pavilion sold teas and ices.

171. One of Kenton's first churches, St Leonard's, Kenton Road which was consecrated in 1927.

172. St Mary's, Kenton replaced St Leonard's as the parish church. The change of dedication came about because the money for the new church came from the sale of St Mary's church, Charing Cross Road. The new church was consecrated by the Bishop of London on 5 December 1936. The old church building was used as a meeting place until it was replaced by a purpose-built hall.

173. As Kenton grew rapidly, there was an increasing need for more places of worship. This is the Methodist church in 1935, eight years after it was built. Other churches in Kenton include All Saints' (1932), St John's (1934) and Kenton Free church (1939). In most cases the existing buildings were erected later than the date of dedication.

174. Old Honeypot Lane at the eastern boundary of Harrow. It was so called due to the road's adhesive qualities in wet weather. In the late 1930s it was completely transformed into a wide highway lined with factories and houses.

175a & b.(above left and right) These two photographs create a remarkable panoramic shot showing the junction with Kenton Road and Kenton Lane in about 1934. The small building on the corner of Kenton Lane is the local office of H.R.P. estates (H.R. and P. (London) Limited). They developed the old St Bartholomew's hospital lands along Kenton Lane and Christchurch Avenue. 'The Ideal home for you ... the hallmark of good housing ... a name that implies sound construction, and tasteful design. £825. Room for a garage, ten minutes from two tube stations.' The shop was a branch of the Express Dairy. At the end of the parade of shops, the long building far right is the telephone exchange.

176. Kenton Road with the *Kenton Plough* beyond the trees and more new shops being built. This picture dates from *c*.1934.

KENTON PARK PARADE FROM ROOF OF CORNWALL HOUSE.

177. The junction of Kenton Lane and Kenton Road showing the H.R.P. estates next to the Express Dairy on the left. Behind the figure on the left is a poster advertising the Cosy cinema in Wealdstone. The shop on the right-hand side of the road is a branch of Pickfords. a well-known bakery chain of this period.

178. Belmont Halt (later Belmont station) opened on the L.M.S. branch line to Stanmore on 12 September 1932 in time to serve the new Davis estate. The estate was developed on the fields seen here in this 1935 picture. The halt was rebuilt as an island platform station in 1937. As the Second World War broke out, Belmont had become a suburb complete with parades (or 'tops') of shops, a branch of F. W. Woolworth and the Essoldo cinema (demolished in 1970).

179. The end of Belmont station, which closed on 3 October 1964. It was the terminus of the line from Wealdstone after the withdrawal of passenger trains to Stanmore Village in 1952.